Sexuality
and the
Young Christian

Sexuality and the Young Christian

Joanne E. De Jonge

BAKER BOOK HOUSE
Grand Rapids, Michigan 49516

ISBN: 0-8010-3009-9

Third printing, October 1996

Formerly published under the title,
A Beautiful Gift: Your Awakening Sexuality

Pat Adamik, Illustrator

Printed in the United States of America

Contents

To Parents and Teachers

Intended for use in a Christian home and/or school, this book is designed to help children, approximately eleven or twelve years old, understand that sex and our sexuality is a beautiful gift from a loving God.

Written from a Christian perspective, this book is based on the premise that we are created in God's image, and that we alone among God's creatures have the capacity to love God, to love others, and to communicate that love in various ways. It is also based on the premise that our bodies are wonderful creations designed by God; every body part and process is good.

This is a happy book. It assumes that Christians regard their sexuality with joy. It emphasizes God's love for us and our love for others. It speaks of God's wonderful care for us and of how he shows his care by setting limits for the use of our sexuality.

This is also a frank book. It assumes that we can be as open when we talk about sex as we can when we talk about other body processes, such as digestion. Correct terms and realistic illustrations are used with the assumption that anything less would indicate embarrassment about a subject which need not be embarrassing. Sexual intercourse is dealt with openly, but is placed within the limits God has imposed on us.

This is a "you"-centered book. It speaks to the child about his or her relationship with God and with others. It does mention the child's relationship to parents (natural, adoptive, and foster parents), but does not dwell on family relationships. Instead, it focuses on the child as an individual.

This book deals with some issues you may consider too mature for an eleven- or twelve-year-old. Abortion, safe sex, birth control, homosexuality, and rape are mentioned and are defined. These issues are discussed daily in the news.

Certainly, our children have been exposed to these terms. Although some eleven- or twelve-year-olds may not be interested in these issues, other children this age are ready for some explanations.

Our children need to have clear information about these issues. They also need to know that all Christians do not share the same point of view on these topics. But most of all our children must know that, despite the distortions brought about by sin, human sexuality is still a good gift from God. That gift must be used according to God's law in a way that reflects love for God and neighbor.

1

This Book Is About . . .

This book is about sex. It's about boys and girls, men and women, love, and making babies.

Maybe you'll giggle when you read this, or you might be embarrassed. Maybe you think that you know everything about sex already and don't need this book. Maybe you've heard friends use some words relating to sex and you wonder what those words mean. On the other hand, you might not yet be interested in sex.

However you react when you read or hear about sex, you're probably quite normal. Many grownups, too, are embarrassed to talk about sex, so they make jokes about it. Others may talk openly about it, but secretly wonder about some things. Many people think a lot about sex. Sex is something important, close, and private to most people. Maybe that's why some people hesitate to talk about it.

God made sex an important and wonderful part of our lives. He created us either male or female, with bodies more complicated than we can imagine. He made animals male and female with complicated bodies too, but he made us in his image. We have the ability to think, to love, and to share. He gave us deep emotions in addition to strong urges and desires. He gave us sex as a beautiful way to love and to share ourselves.

Sex and your sexuality (your femaleness or your maleness) will probably influence much of your life. That's the way God made you. Of course, he gave you many ways to share yourself with others and to show that you care for others. But he added the special gift of sex and your sexuality. When understood and used properly, this special gift can be wonderful.

God didn't promise us that life would always be easy. Growing up can be tough sometimes. Your feelings change, your body changes, your emotions do flip-flops, and you're lost in the middle of it all. It's hard to imagine that others have gone through the same changes and had some of the same feelings. It's also hard to imagine that anyone could think this is all so wonderful.

But you *are* growing up; you can't stop the changes that happen. And you really wouldn't want to, would you? You will become a more mature, sexual person. You'll be able to enjoy one of God's most precious gifts to you.

Do you wonder now just what's happening or about to happen to you? Are you confused about some of the details, or not quite sure that you have all the facts straight? Or don't you quite understand why sex is such a wonderful gift? Then read on.

2

Male Sex Organs

Some people think that a male's sex organs are really quite simple. After all, much of a male's equipment is attached to the outside of his body, where it's easy to see. Most girls have seen a little boy's penis. Any boy knows what his penis looks like, how his scrotum hangs between his legs, and how his testicles, inside his scrotum, feel. There they are. What's so wonderful about them?

What's wonderful is the way all the organs, tubes, and glands work together. Every part was created exactly right to fill a certain purpose, and each part does its work automatically. A sexually excited man doesn't need to remember to open a certain tube or close a certain valve. His body works automatically while he's concentrating on his emotions. He may not think about it at the time, but he's a beautiful example of how wonderfully God created men's bodies.

Testicles

A man's testicles are an example. (Sometimes they're called testes.) They're the little glands which lie inside that sac of skin. They make sperm cells which are needed to make babies. One testicle often hangs a little lower than the other, but that makes no difference in the way they work.

Each testicle in a mature male is only about one and one-half inches long, one inch wide, and less than an inch thick. Yet each testicle is filled with hundreds of thread-like tubes which are tightly coiled together. Although those tubes are as small as threads, they manufacture billions of sperm cells.

You'd think that God would have put testicles inside a body where they would be protected. But he had a good reason for putting them just where he did. Sperm cells are delicate; they will develop only at a certain temperature. Body temperature is too warm. If a man's testicles were inside his body, the sperm would not develop properly.

God created some animals with testicles inside their bodies. But those animals mate only at certain times of the year. During those times, the animals' testicles come out of their bodies to produce sperm cells. When mating season is over, the testicles go back into the bodies and stop producing sperm cells.

God created humans to love each other all the time, not just during certain seasons. So men's testicles always lie outside of their bodies. Of course, people show love in many different ways. But if a man wants to make love sexually, he is able to do so at any time.

Scrotum

The scrotum, that sac of skin which covers the testicles, is another wonder. It acts as a thermostat. In cold weather, the scrotum shrivels and brings the testicles close to the body for heat. In warm weather the scrotum hangs low so that the testicles can lie farther from the warm body. Even when a man pays no attention to it, his scrotum keeps his testicles in just the right place.

Male Sex Organs

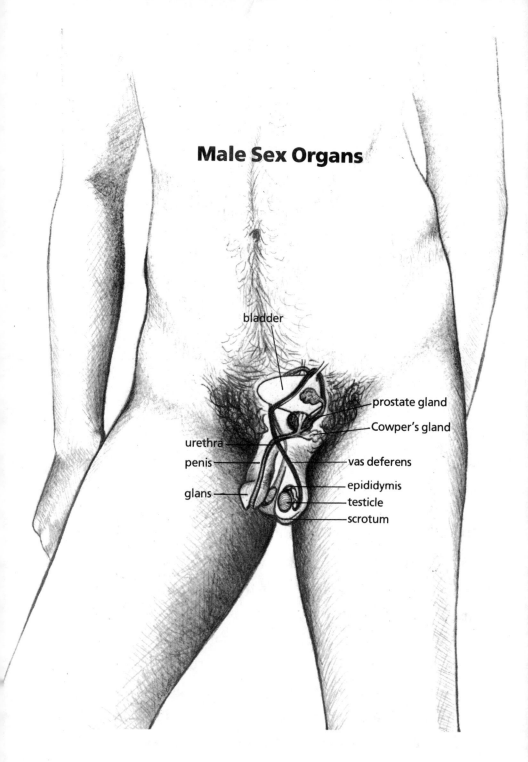

bladder

prostate gland

Cowper's gland

urethra

penis

vas deferens

glans

epididymis

testicle

scrotum

Adult Male Internal Sex Organs

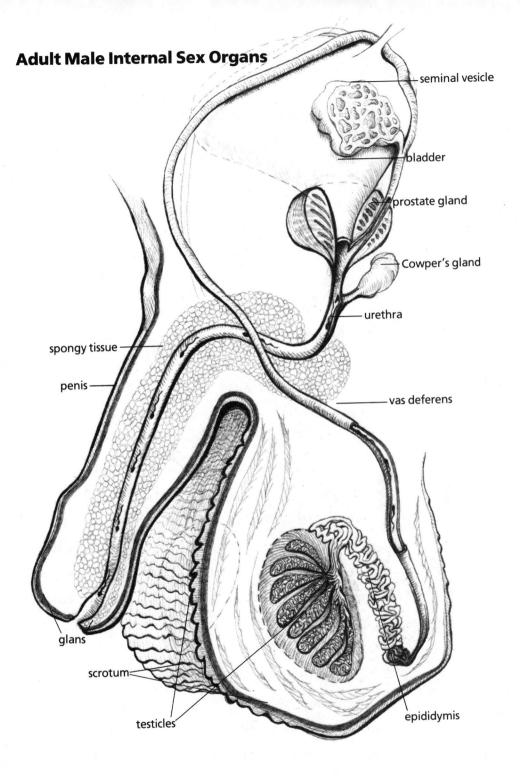

seminal vesicle

bladder

prostate gland

Cowper's gland

urethra

spongy tissue

penis

vas deferens

glans

scrotum

testicles

epididymis

Tubes and Glands

Sperm cells can't stay in the testicles forever. They eventually must find their way out of those thread-like tubes, up through the body, and out of the penis. They follow a complicated system of tubes laced with glands and valves. Each part of the system, of course, has a special purpose.

First, the sperm cells collect in a storage tube behind the testicle. This tube is called the epididymis. This tube also manufactures part of the liquid that sperm swim in. There's an epididymis on each testicle. If the epididymis weren't there, the sperm might be left high and dry, with no place to gather and not much to swim in.

From this storage tube the sperm swim in their liquid through a tube called the vas deferens. This is the connecting link between the testicle and the final tube that runs through the penis. One vas deferens runs up from each testicle, over the bladder, and connects with that final tube.

Two little glands called seminal vesicles open into these connecting links. One seminal vesicle opens into each vas deferens. These glands pour a little more liquid into the tubes so the sperm

Sexuality and the Young Christian

can swim better. All this liquid with sperm in it is called semen.

A muscular gland called the prostate surrounds the end of the vas deferens. The prostate adds more fluid to the semen. It also stores sperm cells, allowing them and the fluid to mix more thoroughly.

Two little glands called Cowper's glands lie just below the prostate. They secrete a small amount of fluid which lubricates the urethra.

The urethra is the final tube through the penis. It carries both urine and semen. Urine and semen don't mix in the urethra. The passage to the bladder is always blocked when a penis is erect and spurting out semen.

All these tubes and glands sound complicated. They are, but they work well. They were created so that a man doesn't have to think about where to send his sperm. They automatically go from the testicles to the penis by the right route.

Penis

The penis is made of spongy tissues. Usually it hangs soft and limp.

No two penises are exactly alike. Size varies, exact shape may vary a little, and even the place of the opening at the end may vary. None of these variations affect how a penis operates. A small penis and a large penis work equally well. There's a variety of penises, just as there's a variety of fingers and noses, but all are normal.

A penis is shaped somewhat like a finger and is about one and one-half to four inches long (when it is limp). It has a smooth rounded head (glans) from which the urine and semen come out.

Circumcision

When a boy is born, the end of his penis is covered with a loose flap of skin called the foreskin. This makes the whole penis look like a smooth tube, because the head isn't exposed. The foreskin can be pulled back so that the head of the penis shows.

Doctors often will cut away the foreskin in a minor operation called circumcision. Then the head of the penis is easier to keep clean. Both circumcised and uncircumcised penises work equally well.

During Old Testament times God commanded the Jews to circumcise their sons. That was a sign that they were God's special people. Christians today don't regard circumcision as a reli-

Circumcision

Circumcision affects only the appearance of the penis, not its function.

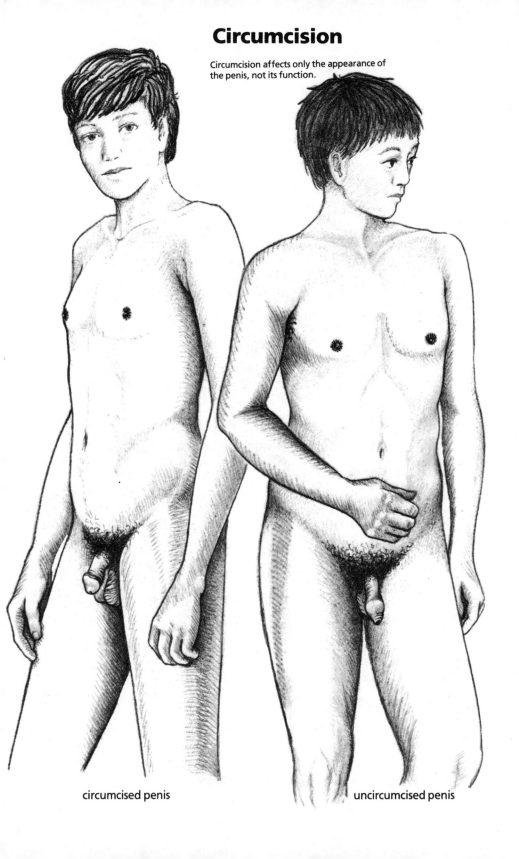

circumcised penis

uncircumcised penis

gious rite. Many people have their little boys circumcised simply because it's easier to keep the circumcised penis clean.

Erection

A penis has the amazing ability to change from a soft, limp organ used for urinating to a firm, erect one used for releasing semen. This can happen quickly. Blood rushes into arteries in the soft spongy tissue. As the arteries fill with blood, the penis swells, becomes hard, and stands up and away from the body. This is called an erection.

Men and boys have erections for all sorts of reasons. Thinking about sex or having something touch or rub the penis can cause an erection. Sometimes an erection will happen for no obvious reason. Often a male can wake up in the morning with an erection.

Sometimes the erection lasts only a few minutes. The blood drains away and the penis becomes limp again.

If a male is sexually excited, the erection may last until he has released his semen. This may happen quite fast. But if the man is making love, he can keep his erection and his semen for a longer time to extend the pleasure of lovemaking.

When a man has an erection, the passage to his bladder is automatically closed. The penis is then used for spurting semen.

Semen usually spurts out of the penis with quite a bit of force. This spurting is called an ejaculation.

An erection followed by an ejaculation is often called a climax or an orgasm. An orgasm is generally a good, pleasurable feeling.

The real wonder of erection and ejaculation lies in how beautifully the whole male system works together. A man doesn't have to think about directing blood to his penis, controlling his bladder, or spurting out his semen. All of this happens automatically, at the right time and in the right order.

So you see, a man's sex organs are not at all simple. They're a complicated system of organs, tubes, and glands that all must work together perfectly. God created this system to work just right all by itself.

Female Sex Organs

Awoman's sex organs are far less visible than a man's. Most of a woman's organs are tucked away safely inside her body, but that doesn't make them any more mysterious or any less amazing. Her organs were also created to do exactly the right work at exactly the right time.

Ovaries

A grown woman probably doesn't think much about her ovaries. They're out of sight and they usually work well all by themselves. Yet they are amazing little glands.

Each ovary in a mature female is about the size and shape of an unshelled almond, approximately one inch long. A young girl's ovaries are smaller. They grow as a girl matures sexually.

Each ovary holds thousands of egg cells. Egg cells are called ova. One egg cell is called an ovum.

Ova are tiny, smaller than a pinpoint. But they're necessary for making babies. One ovum, if it has been fertilized by a sperm cell, can begin to divide and eventually become a baby.

Every normal girl baby already has, when she's born, thousands of these tiny ova in each ovary. Boys aren't born with sperm cells. Their bodies begin to make sperm when they become sexually mature. But a girl is born with all the ova her body will produce.

Each ovum doesn't automatically become a baby. The cells must ripen and one must meet a sperm, but each of those tiny ova within that baby does hold the possibility for becoming another person. Every normal female holds within her ovaries thousands of tiny seeds of life.

Ova don't stay in a woman's ovaries forever. As they mature, or ripen, they travel one at a time to her uterus. To reach her uterus, they must pass through the fallopian tubes.

Fallopian Tubes

Look carefully at the illustrations on the next two pages. One end of each fallopian tube opens directly into the uterus. But the other, ruffled end doesn't open directly into an ovary. It doesn't even touch the ovary; it just lies close. Yet, when an ovum leaves an ovary, it always finds its way into the fallopian tube. Exactly how this happens remains a mystery.

Each fallopian tube has little hairs, or cilia, on its inside lining. These cilia begin beating after an ovum is released from an ovary. As soon as the ovum is inside the fallopian tube, the beating cilia guide it toward the uterus.

A woman can't control the cilia in her fallopian tubes. In fact, she usually can hardly feel when an ovum is released from her ovary, so she wouldn't know when to start the cilia beating. Yet the cilia beat automatically at the right time, so the ovum moves through her tube to her uterus.

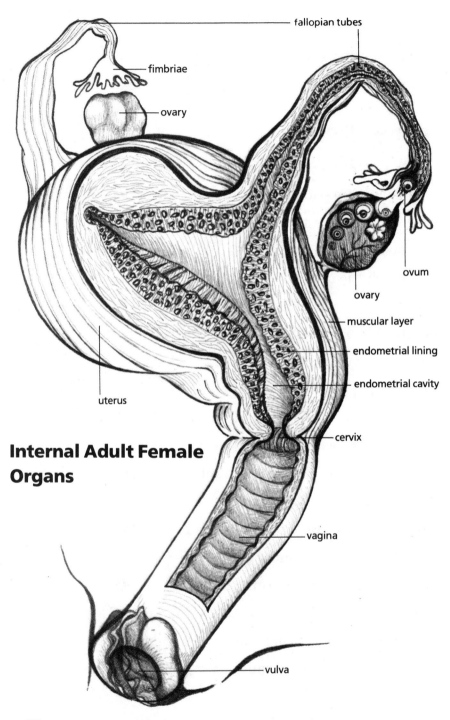

fallopian tubes

fimbriae

ovary

ovum

ovary

muscular layer

endometrial lining

endometrial cavity

uterus

cervix

Internal Adult Female Organs

vagina

vulva

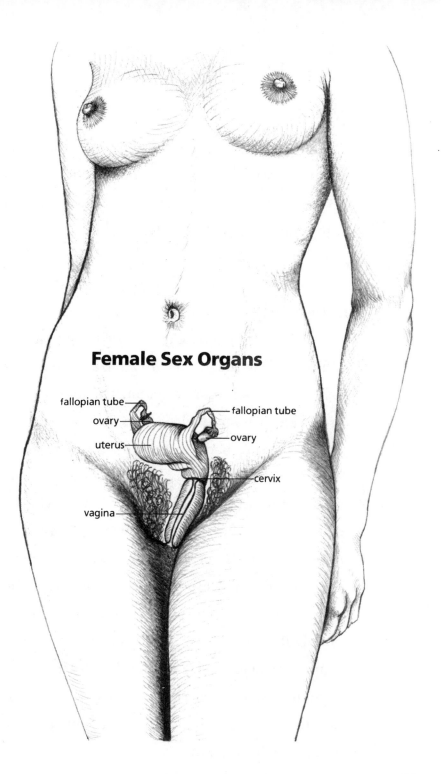

Female Sex Organs

fallopian tube

fallopian tube

ovary

ovary

uterus

cervix

vagina

Uterus

The uterus is normally about the size and shape of an upside-down pear. The bottom part—where the stem would be on the pear—is a muscular section called the cervix.

It's in the uterus that a fertilized ovum develops into a baby. Then, of course, the uterus stretches to the size of the baby. Often a uterus is called a womb, especially if a baby is developing in it.

The walls of the uterus are amazing. The outer layers are elastic and muscular. The inner layers are filled with many blood vessels.

Most of our body organs aren't capable of stretching very far, but the walls of the uterus were created to stretch without harm when a baby is developing. When the baby is ready to be born, the muscles of the uterine wall automatically contract to help push the baby out of the uterus. Then the uterus shrinks to approximately its normal size. (It will be slightly larger than it was before the woman had a baby.) If a woman has never carried a baby in her uterus, the uterus remains about the size and shape of an upside-down pear.

Sexuality and the Young Christian

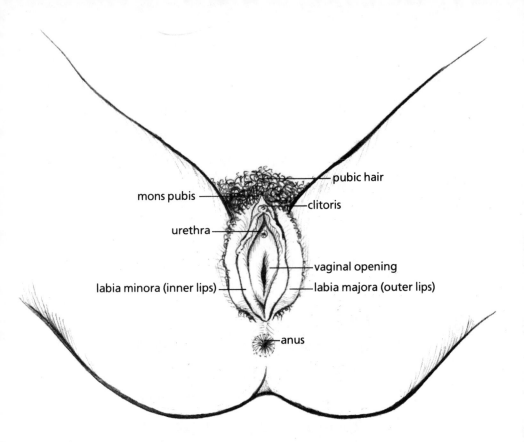

labels: pubic hair, mons pubis, clitoris, urethra, vaginal opening, labia minora (inner lips), labia majora (outer lips), anus

Female External Genitals—Vulva

Vagina

The cervix (the bottom of the uterus) opens into the vagina, a tube that leads out of a woman's body. This is the passage through which a baby comes when it is born.

The walls of the vagina are much like the uterine walls. They're muscular and stretchy. The vagina can stretch wide enough to make room for a baby. Usually the vagina is less than an inch wide.

The vagina is also the passage through which sperm swim to meet an ovum. Because it can stretch so easily, a vagina can fit around a penis of any size.

Vulva

The end of the vagina opposite the uterus opens between the legs, and is covered with folds of flesh called the vulva. This is the only part of a girl's sex organs that you can see, and it looks simply like a little slit. Actually, the vulva is much more complicated than a simple split. (See page 33.)

There are really two folds of skin, overlapped for double protection of the delicate organs inside. We usually call these folds the outer lips and the inner lips.

At the front of the vulva, where the two sets of lips meet, rests a smooth knob called the clitoris. The clitoris in grown women is about the size of a small cherry pit, and contains many nerves and blood vessels. When a woman becomes sexually excited, her clitoris swells up a bit and becomes especially sensitive. Doctors can find no function for the clitoris besides that of giving a woman especially good sensations. Isn't it interesting that God gave a woman a body part purely for pleasure when she makes love?

Directly behind the clitoris, also beneath the outer and inner lips, lies an opening called the urethra. This is not connected to the vagina. Instead, it's connected to a tube which comes from the bladder. Urine comes out of the body through the urethra.

Behind the urethra lies the opening to the vagina. It's usually just called the vaginal opening. In young girls, the vaginal opening is partially covered by a piece of skin called the hymen. As a girl becomes older, her hymen is often stretched or torn while she is exercising or playing. Occasionally a woman will have a doctor cut her hymen before she is married. Sexual intercourse can be painful for a woman at first if her hymen covers part of her vagina.

Just inside the vaginal opening lie two pinprick-sized holes that lead to glands. These glands, called Bartholin's glands, produce a mucus. When a woman becomes sexually excited, these glands begin to work. They help make her vagina wet and slightly slippery.

When these glands begin to work, more blood flows into the walls of the woman's vagina and into her clitoris. The whole vaginal area becomes a little swollen, wet, and sensitive. Then the vagina can fit comfortably around a penis.

A woman's sexual equipment is as right for her as a man's is for him. She doesn't have to turn on her glands or direct her blood flow. Everything happens automatically at the right time. A woman, like a man, can concentrate on the pleasures of making love.

Menstruation

A woman's body also automatically prepares itself for the growth of a baby inside her uterus. This is one of the most complicated and delicate processes that takes place inside a human body. It involves many hormones (chemical messages) which are poured into the blood at certain times. It also involves delicate timing between a woman's ovaries and uterus.

Usually a woman's ovaries release one ovum every twenty-eight days. This is called ovulation. In some women this timing is different. Some women ovulate once every twenty-six days or perhaps every thirty days. Ovulation may even be irregular. But in all women the sequence of events is the same. The ovaries usually take turns. First the left will release an ovum; the next time the right ovary will.

While an ovum is maturing, or growing bigger, within an ovary, the woman's uterus is preparing a special lining. This lining is soft and cushiony, filled with blood cells. A fertilized ovum can attach itself to this lining and develop into a baby.

When the ovum is mature, it breaks out of the ovary and makes its way to the fallopian tube. Inside the tube, cilia push the ovum toward the uterus.

While the ovum is in the fallopian tube, messages are sent, by means of hormones, between the tubes and the waiting uterus. If the ovum is fertilized while it is in the tube, the uterus is "told" that the soft cushiony lining is needed. So it stays in place.

If the ovum is not fertilized, the uterus is "told" that no baby will develop. The lining is not needed. Automatically it breaks apart and rinses out of the woman's body through her vagina. Then her uterus is clean and ready to build another lining.

The unfertilized ovum breaks apart as it travels through the tube to the uterus. It is also rinsed out of the woman's body with the unused lining.

Female Sex Organs   37

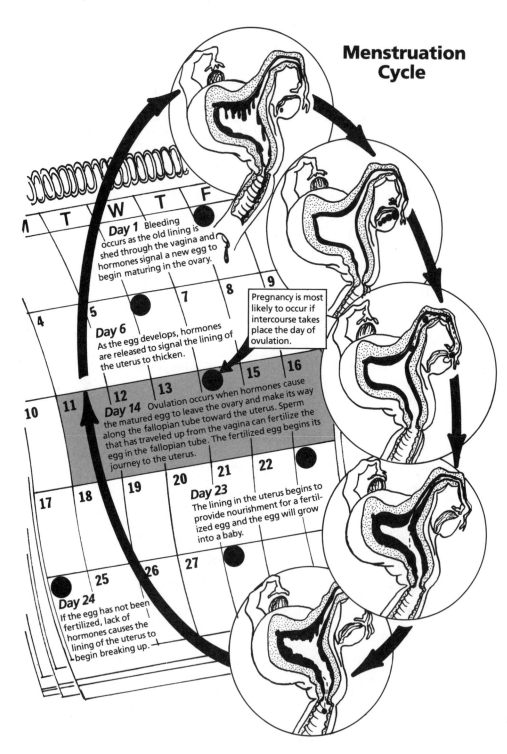

Menstruation Cycle

Day 1 Bleeding occurs as the old lining is shed through the vagina and hormones signal a new egg to begin maturing in the ovary.

Day 6 As the egg develops, hormones are released to signal the lining of the uterus to thicken.

Pregnancy is most likely to occur if intercourse takes place the day of ovulation.

Day 14 Ovulation occurs when hormones cause the matured egg to leave the ovary and make its way along the fallopian tube toward the uterus. Sperm that has traveled up from the vagina can fertilize the egg in the fallopian tube. The fertilized egg begins its journey to the uterus.

Day 23 The lining in the uterus begins to provide nourishment for a fertilized egg and the egg will grow into a baby.

Day 24 If the egg has not been fertilized, lack of hormones causes the lining of the uterus to begin breaking up.

The shedding of the extra uterine lining is called menstruation. It happens about once every month. A woman will often say that she has her period when she is menstruating. Her body is simply shedding those unneeded blood vessels and tissues that lined her uterus. For a few days she seems to be bleeding from her vagina.

Usually, as soon as one lining has been completely shed, the uterus begins to prepare another, and an ovum begins to mature in an ovary. The process begins again. Every month a woman's uterus prepares a clean new lining, just in case an ovum will be fertilized. If the ovum is not fertilized, the woman menstruates.

A girl usually begins to menstruate between the ages of nine and fifteen. From that time until she is about fifty years old, her body is constantly preparing new uterine linings. An intricate process, delicately timed, repeats itself approximately every month. A woman doesn't have to remember to ripen an ovum or to line her uterus. God created her finely tuned body to do that automatically. Her menstrual cycle is an indication that her body is working exactly as God planned.

Sexual Intercourse

Intercourse is communication between people. Sexual intercourse is a special form of communication between a man and a woman, using their sex organs. Sometimes we refer to sexual intercourse as making love.

When a man becomes sexually excited, his penis becomes firm and erect. When a woman becomes sexually excited, her vagina becomes moist and sensitive.

When both a man and a woman are sexually excited, the man slips his penis into the woman's vagina. He may move it in and out a bit and become still more excited. After a few minutes he

41

has an orgasm and semen spurts out of his penis into the woman's vagina. The woman may have an orgasm too, but she doesn't spurt anything out. She just has a wonderful sensation that's hard to describe. Soon after his orgasm, the man's penis becomes soft and limp again.

When a man and a woman are making love, they are as close as two people can be. Not only their bodies, but also their minds and their emotions are centered on each other and the way they are expressing their love. Sexual intercourse is one of the most wonderful experiences a person can have physically, emotionally, and mentally.

Because sexual intercourse is such an intimate expression of love, God gave us some guidelines for using it. He has told us in the Bible that we should not commit adultery or fornication. Adultery is sexual intercourse with someone other than your husband or wife if you are married. Fornication is sexual intercourse with anyone, if you are not married. God wants husbands and wives to make love with each other, not with others. He wants us to save sexual intercourse for the person we marry.

Our ability to love and care deeply is part of God's image in us. It sets us apart from all other creatures. The ability to make love—not just have sex—is also a reflection of God's image. It involves our inner selves, our emotions and feelings, as well as our bodies. A person who "makes love" just for sexual excitement is lying about his or her inner feelings. Lying to another person about love and commitment can hurt that person more than almost anything else. That's why God gave us guidelines for sexual intercourse. He doesn't want us to hurt ourselves or others by using the gift of our sexuality too freely. When used as God intended, making love is a beautiful and exciting experience.

Sexual intercourse is also a wonderful physical experience. Both men and women have parts of their bodies, especially around their sex organs, that are especially sensitive. They become sexually excited if these areas are touched. Some people become sexually excited by just thinking about sex. This excitement builds up and then is released during an orgasm. It's a feeling that can't be described. Isn't it delightful that God created us to have such a good physical experience while we're making love?

Sexual intercourse also makes babies. A man's semen contains millions of living sperm cells.

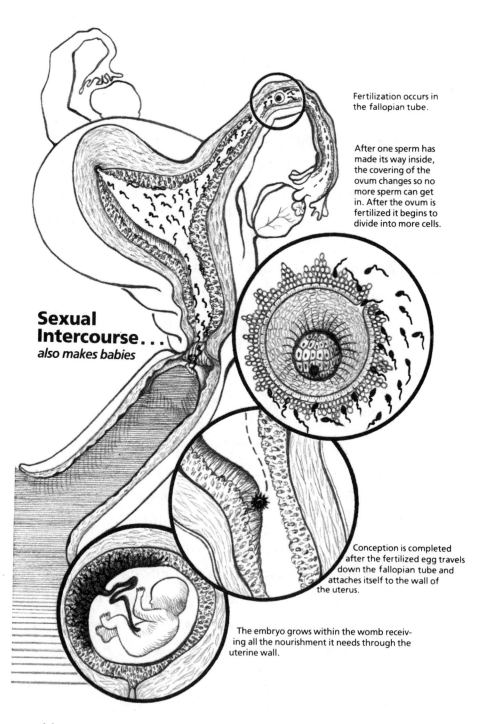

Fertilization occurs in the fallopian tube.

After one sperm has made its way inside, the covering of the ovum changes so no more sperm can get in. After the ovum is fertilized it begins to divide into more cells.

Sexual Intercourse...
also makes babies

Conception is completed after the fertilized egg travels down the fallopian tube and attaches itself to the wall of the uterus.

The embryo grows within the womb receiving all the nourishment it needs through the uterine wall.

44

When semen is spurted into a woman's vagina, sperm begin swimming toward her uterus. Some swim right on up into her fallopian tubes. If a living ovum is in one of her tubes, the sperm are attracted to it and crowd around it. One sperm wiggles its way into the ovum. Then the ovum is fertilized and begins to divide. Eventually a baby is formed. When a woman has a baby forming inside of her, we say that she is pregnant.

Only one sperm cell can fertilize an ovum. After it has made its way inside, the covering of the ovum changes so that no more sperm cells can get in.

The rest of the sperm cells die within forty-eight hours. They, and the liquid part of the semen, generally seep back out of the vagina.

A woman doesn't become pregnant every time she makes love. Sometimes there is no ovum in either of her fallopian tubes. Sometimes the ovum has already died and is beginning to fall apart. Her ovum and the man's sperm cell must be in just the right place at just the right time if she is going to become pregnant.

Many animals have sexual intercourse only to reproduce. The female often has no interest in a male unless she can become pregnant right then.

God created people different from animals. Men and women are always interested in each other. They don't make love only to make babies. They have sexual intercourse also to express a deep love for each other and for a wonderful physical experience. God gave us a special gift in sex and our sexuality. It is a gift which we should use, with joy, within his guidelines.

5

Becoming an Adult

Becoming an adult may be the farthest thing from your mind right now. Perhaps you're not at all interested in how adults make love or how you will change sexually to become an adult.

If that's the way you feel, you're perfectly normal. Lots of people your age feel exactly the same way.

On the other hand, maybe you are very interested in information about sex. Maybe you know something, but not everything, about sex. Perhaps you've heard people talking about sex and wondered what all the fuss is about.

If you feel that way, you're perfectly normal also. Lots of people your age feel the same way you do.

How can you be so normal and yet so different from other people your age? That's one of the wonders of being a person and not just a thing.

When God creates people, he makes every one different from everyone else. Each person has his or her special interests and abilities. Each person has his or her own mind, conscience, and soul. God creates each person in his image and gives that person the ability to love. Yet each person is unique and expresses that love in his or her own way.

God knows us as individuals. He doesn't just love people in general; he loves each of us. He doesn't love you because you're sort of like Sara or Philip. He loves you because you're you.

We're all different outside as well as inside. We're different colors, heights, weights, shapes, and sizes. We have different hair, noses, and mouths. The list could go on and on.

We also all become adults at different times. Some young children seem adult in the way they think and act. Some adults seem to never mature in their feelings or actions. Some people's bodies become adult when they're quite young. Others take their time about becoming adult. Some people want to grow up quickly; other people don't care.

But one way that we're all alike is that we all have human bodies. God created these bodies to become adult in a certain way. Just as we all breathe in about the same way, and we all digest our food in about the same way, so we all become adult in about the same way. *When* this happens to you and *precisely how long it will take* depends on the timetable God has set inside your body.

So, whether or not you are interested right now in how you will change, you know that you *will* become an adult. Certain changes will take place, probably over the next few years, within your body.

Common Changes

There are certain changes common to both girls and boys. Most of these are "inside" changes, changes in emotions and feelings. Sometimes these changes can be fun; other times they can be confusing and almost frightening.

When your body begins to turn on its adult "switches," certain hormones begin to flow into your blood. New hormones often affect your moods. That's why, when you are an adolescent (in the process of becoming an adult), you have so many ups and downs. One day you may love the world and everyone in it; the next day you may feel like growling at everyone. One day you may be sure of yourself; the next day you may feel that the whole world is against you. Sometimes you don't even understand yourself.

It takes your body a while to adjust to the new hormones and to the process of growing up. All those mood changes are signs that your sex hormones are beginning to flow. Your ups and downs are your body's way of telling you that you are beginning to become an adult. They won't last forever. When your body becomes accustomed to the changes it's undergoing, your moods and emotions will settle down.

Besides pouring new hormones into your blood, your body also begins to produce its adult layer of lubricant. Your skin, especially on your face, neck, and shoulders, becomes more oily. This can be embarrassing at first, because you're likely to get pimples, also called acne. It takes your skin time to adjust. Usually the acne disappears after a while. Meanwhile, it is another indication that you are becoming an adult.

You probably will notice that you are perspiring more, especially under your arms. That's a sign that some of your glands are waking up.

Your voice will also begin to change. If you are a girl, your voice will become just a little deeper and fuller. You will begin to sound more like a woman and less like a little girl.

If you are a boy, your voice will change drastically. For a while you may have trouble with your voice "cracking" or "squeaking." Your vocal cords will be trying to adjust to a new spurt of growth. Finally your voice will deepen, and you'll sound like a man.

You'll probably notice many changes in your body. If you're a girl, you'll begin to look more like a woman. If you're a boy, you'll begin to look more like a man. Let's take some of these changes step by step.

Becoming a Woman

If you're a girl, you may notice that your breasts are beginning to develop. Sometimes one breast becomes slightly larger than the other; then the second one catches up. Many women

Breast Changes of Puberty

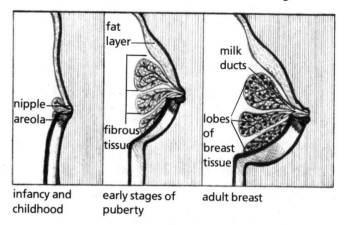

infancy and childhood

early stages of puberty

adult breast

have one breast which is slightly larger than the other.

Some girls' breasts begin to develop when they're nine or ten. Other girls may wait until they're fourteen or fifteen.

Not all women's breasts are the same size. Some women have small breasts while other women develop very large breasts.

When a woman has a baby, her breasts produce milk for that baby. Both large and small breasts produce the right milk for the baby, so size doesn't make any difference in function.

You'll probably also grow taller. In fact, you may suddenly find that you're the tallest person in your class. Others may not have had their growth spurt yet.

You may also notice that you're gaining weight in different parts of your body. Your face may become fuller; your upper arms may fatten a bit. Your hips and thighs become broader, and it seems that you have more of a waistline. Women's hips are generally quite wide. A woman's pelvis is broader than a man's. This allows room for a baby to be born.

You will also grow more hair. You might notice an increase of hair on your arms and legs. Hair might begin to grow under your arms. Many women have hair on their arms and legs and under their arms. Some have more hair than others. Some have none.

You'll also notice hair beginning to grow around your vulva, in your pubic region. This is pubic hair and is generally coarser than the hair on your head or arms. Women have a triangular patch of pubic hair. Some women have more pubic hair than others.

You may not notice at this point, but your genitals (your outer and inner lips, clitoris) become a little darker in color and a little fleshier. They're preparing for your adult sexual life.

The landmark that you'll notice is the beginning of menstruation, your first period. This, too, hap-

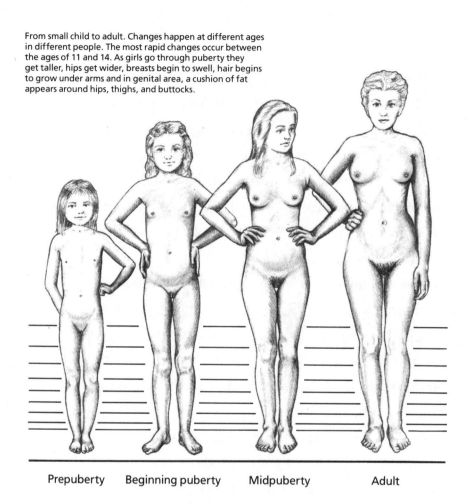

From small child to adult. Changes happen at different ages in different people. The most rapid changes occur between the ages of 11 and 14. As girls go through puberty they get taller, hips get wider, breasts begin to swell, hair begins to grow under arms and in genital area, a cushion of fat appears around hips, thighs, and buttocks.

| Prepuberty | Beginning puberty | Midpuberty | Adult |

Puberty in Girls

pens at different times in different girls. It can come when you are nine, or it can wait until you're fifteen or sixteen. Any time it comes is right for you.

A girl's period isn't always regular at first. Your body may take a few months to become reg-

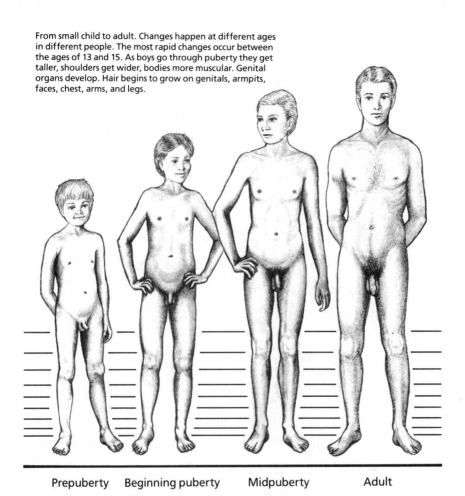

From small child to adult. Changes happen at different ages in different people. The most rapid changes occur between the ages of 13 and 15. As boys go through puberty they get taller, shoulders get wider, bodies more muscular. Genital organs develop. Hair begins to grow on genitals, armpits, faces, chest, arms, and legs.

Prepuberty   Beginning puberty   Midpuberty   Adult

Puberty in Boys

ular about releasing its ova. You may have a period and then wait a few months until the next one. Eventually your body will settle down into its own individual rhythm.

Your body already has its own individual rhythm. That's why you may have had some but not all of these changes. Or you may have had none. Maybe you've had your period, but nothing else has changed. Or maybe your breasts have begun to develop but you haven't had your period. Some girls begin to change when they are nine or ten. Others don't begin until they are thirteen, fourteen, or fifteen. Whatever is happening to you is right for your body. You will become a woman by the timetable God has set inside of you.

Becoming a Man

If you're a boy, you may notice that your arms and legs are becoming thicker. You're developing muscles. Some men have very muscular arms and legs; others don't. However you develop, you *will* have bigger muscles in your arms and legs than you had as a boy.

Your shoulders will begin to broaden, too. You may find that your shirts don't fit as well as they did. That's because your shoulders are becoming broad, like a man's.

You'll also notice that both your penis and your testicles are growing larger, and your penis is becoming a little darker. Your sex organs are preparing to make semen. Some penises grow larger than others, but all eventually release semen. Size makes no difference.

You'll notice that you're growing more hair. You may grow more hair on your arms and legs. Hair might begin to grow under your arms and maybe even on your chest.

Many men have hair on their arms, legs, and under their arms. Some have more hair than others. Some have none. Some men have a lot of hair on their chest; some have none. It's hard to tell ahead of time what you'll have. Whatever you have is normal for you.

Sooner or later you'll begin to grow whiskers on your face. Usually that starts with a little "peach fuzz" on your upper lip and maybe on your chin. Some men develop heavy beards on their cheeks. Others have light whiskers around their mouths and chins. Many boys don't develop beards until they're about eighteen. Others will when they are in their early teens. Again, whatever type of beard you develop and when you develop it is normal for you.

You'll also notice hair beginning to grow in your pubic region, around your penis and testicles. This pubic hair is generally coarser than the rest of your body hair. All men have pubic hair. Some have more than others.

The landmark you'll notice is your first ejaculation. You've probably had erections before, but usually nothing else has happened. Some day, you may notice that your penis is especially sensitive when you touch or rub it. This time, instead of having only an erection, you suddenly have a super-good sensation and some fluid spurts out. This is your first ejaculation, and it's an indication that your body is now making sperm cells.

Usually a boy's semen is slightly sticky and clear. Later, as your body makes more sperm, the semen will become milky and thick.

You may find that you have an erection and ejaculation in your sleep. You might have a dream about girls or about something else sexual. When you wake up you'll find that you've spurted out some semen. You may feel like you've wet the bed, but you haven't. You've had a wet dream (also called a nocturnal emission). Almost all males have wet dreams. They're the body's way of disposing of some sperm before it makes more. Wet dreams are simply ejaculations which happen when a male is sleeping.

After you have had your first ejaculation, your body will continue to make sperm for the rest of your life. Your ejaculations are signs that, sexually, you are a man.

Maybe you are already becoming a man. Maybe you've had some but not all of the changes. Perhaps you've noticed that your penis is growing, but you don't have any hair under your arms. Maybe you've had an ejaculation but your muscles haven't changed much. Some boys begin to change when they are eleven or twelve. Others don't begin until they are fourteen or fifteen. Whatever is happening to you is right for your body. You will become a man by the timetable God has set inside of you.

Becoming an Adult Inside

All these physical changes we've talked about are only that—physical changes. Our society places far too much emphasis on what a person looks like. Television and magazines give us the impression that a man should be very muscular or a woman should have big breasts. This is nonsense. However you develop is fine. After all, what a person is like inside is far more important than what he or she looks like.

You may be changing, physically, faster than some of your classmates, or you may not be changing at all yet. But these physical changes don't tell the whole story. You are also changing inside, in your thoughts and emotions. Nobody can see that and nobody can chart that for you. Sometimes, the inside changes are the hardest part of growing up. Especially when your hormones first begin to flow, growing up inside as well as outside may be difficult.

But you *are* growing up. You are a unique person and are developing into a unique adult. God has a plan for your adult life, just as he has a timetable for your body. He knows and cares about how you are growing up inside.

It's nice to know, as you become an adult, that all other adults went through the same physical changes. But it's especially nice to know that there's another Person who cares about all of your growing up, the inside as well as the outside.

You and Others

So far we've talked about you and the changes you can look forward to. We haven't said much about how those changes may affect your attitude toward other people.

As you begin to grow up inside, you naturally begin to think differently about some people. Possibly you act differently around them. You're becoming an adult, so you're beginning to act more like an adult.

Many times you'll probably just want to be a kid. Other times you may feel capable of behaving as an adult. Maybe you have no interest in becoming an adult yet. That's fine. Don't rush it.

Gradually, you'll find yourself thinking and feeling more like an adult, and that will affect the people around you.

You and the Opposite Sex

How do you feel about the opposite sex? Maybe you still feel that boys or girls are weird. You wouldn't go near them, even if someone paid you. You're not sure why, but you'd just as soon stay away from them.

Have you become "boy crazy" or "girl crazy" lately? Perhaps you've recently discovered that your friends of the opposite sex are attractive. You'd really like to make a special impression on them simply because they *are* the opposite sex.

Maybe some of your friends are boys and some are girls. You really don't care what sex they are. You simply like them as people.

However you feel about the opposite sex, you're normal for your age.

You probably *know* that members of the opposite sex really aren't weird. In fact, some boys or girls are really quite nice. But you don't have to be interested in them right now. Many people your age aren't. If you feel as if boys or girls are strange creatures, it's probably a sign that, deep inside, something is telling you that there *is* a difference between you and them. Don't be surprised when you begin to like that difference.

If you're "boy crazy" or "girl crazy," that's a signal that your sex hormones have begun to flow. You're beginning to sense your sexuality. There *is* something especially appealing about members of the opposite sex. They *are* fun to be with.

Adults feel that attraction, too. They like to be with members of the opposite sex because they *are* the opposite sex. Some feel that attraction more than others. It's part of their sex drive, and some people have stronger sex drives than others.

Most adults have learned that this attraction can be pleasant and can make life interesting. They also have learned to use their sexuality within the bounds that God has placed. They reserve intimate sexual expressions for the person they marry. Yet they enjoy their sexuality and the way it colors their lives.

You're just beginning to feel your sexuality. You probably have a long way to go before you'll know how to handle your feelings. There's no rush; you have a lot of learning to do. Enjoy it. Your sexuality is a beautiful gift from God. When it's understood and used properly, your sexuality can color your whole life beautifully.

If you have both girlfriends and boyfriends, that's great. After all, inside, people are people, and you may have interests in common with both boys and girls. As you grow up, you'll probably have friends from both sexes. That's as it should be. You'll be richer for it.

Men and women have friends from both sexes, too. Although sexuality influences adults' lives, it doesn't control everything they do. Many people like to be with certain other people simply for friendship and common interests. They care about other people and want to know how those people think and feel. Friendships should never be restricted to the members of your own sex.

Dreams and Daydreams

You may find yourself dreaming about certain people more now than you used to. When you're asleep, those dreams may just pop into your head. They can be exciting, or they can even be embarrassing. That's normal. Lots of people would never think of telling another soul about some of their dreams. Maybe your body is "waking up" and trying to figure out for itself what to do with these new feelings. Perhaps you don't think about some of these things during the day, so they just come out in dreams at night. Maybe you do think about these things during the day and also dream about them at night. Whatever the case, don't worry; everybody dreams.

Maybe you daydream about a certain person a lot. Do you have a "crush" on someone? Lots of people, especially people with active imaginations, day-dream a lot. Lots of people have "crushes" on other people.

Daydreaming can be fun, as long as you realize that daydreams are just that—dreams. A "crush" usually doesn't blossom into a romance. Don't become too involved, thinking that daydreams could be real. You could set yourself up for some disappointments that way. That doesn't mean that you should try to stop daydreaming. Enjoy your imagination within reason.

Curiosity

You've probably had your curiosity satisfied by now. Girls know how boys are made, and boys know what girls look like.

But you may also wonder how certain friends are developing. It's natural to wonder. It's probably also natural to daydream about it a bit. But there are certain things people like to keep private, and they should be kept private. After all, there are certain things you like to keep private, too. Everyone is entitled to personal privacy.

That doesn't mean that you have to stay away from the opposite sex. You'll begin to feel some attractions and that's fine, within decent limits. Enjoy those attractions and enjoy your friendships. There are some pretty wonderful people, both male and female. Friends of either sex are quite special.

You and Adults

You've probably heard people tell you many times to stay away from strangers who are overly friendly. You've been warned for a good reason.

Some adults like to play, sexually, with children. They may like to undress children, handle a child's sex organs, or just harm a child in some way. That's called molesting.

Sometimes an adult will force another adult or a child to have sexual intercourse with him or her. That's called rape. Rape isn't at all pretty or nice to think about, but it does happen.

Sometimes an adult will have sexual intercourse with a person who is related to him or her. That's called incest. A relative might handle a child's sex organs and then tell the child not to tell anyone. This should not happen. Someone must be told.

You may have heard the term "sexual abuse." All of the acts mentioned above fall into that category. Sexual abuse can happen to adults as well as children. But children are often threatened into silence or told that the abuse is not wrong. Sexual abuse *is* wrong; no one may sexually abuse you.

The world isn't perfect. Some adults have had a hard time growing up. Maybe something happened to them that was too much for them to cope with, or maybe they're just sick inside. Those people seem to have sex, love, hate, and caring all mixed up in their minds.

You may meet one of those people some time. If an adult whom you know or whom you don't know doesn't respect your personal privacy, stay away from that person. Tell an adult who really cares for you.

Your body is your own. It's good and decent the way God made it. No adult may take advantage of you because you're young. No adult may talk or force you into any kind of sexual activity with him or her. You are still *you* and are entitled to your own privacy and your own decency. No adult may handle your sex organs or tamper with your body just because he or she is an adult and you are not.

Of course, there are adults who care for you and are rearing you. That's different. They've shown for years that they love you. But they respect your privacy, too. That's part of loving you. They want to help you grow up. If you are a girl, they may help you with your first period or help you buy your first bra. If you are a boy, they may like to know about your first wet dream or tease you about being "girl crazy." But they never would tamper with your body. You are a precious gift to them. They love you and respect you as a person.

You and Your Family

Perhaps you live in a family with a mother, father, sisters, and brothers. Maybe you're an only child, or have one parent, foster parents, or adoptive parents. There are probably many families like yours and many families that are a lot different from yours. There are all sorts of families. That doesn't mean that one kind of family is better than another.

What's important to you is the people you are living with. They're your family. The adults care about you enough to take care of you and assume responsibility for you. Maybe they're not your original parents, but because of the love and care they give you, they are, now, your mother and/or father.

Do you sometimes think that your family doesn't understand you or how you feel? Do you feel that you're alone, not really a part of your family? Maybe you want to talk to other family members or maybe you want to keep to yourself. You may change from day to day. Through it all, you may think that no one in your family knows the real you or understands what's happening to you.

That's a normal part of growing up. Your hormones are beginning to flow and your moods sometimes change wildly. You're beginning to think for yourself, and sometimes you question the way your parents think. All these mood changes coupled with the questionings can be fun, but they can also be difficult.

Maybe it will help you to remember that the adult(s) in your family went through the same changes that you face. They probably understand more than you think they do. And they probably care much more than you think they do. Sometimes they can be surprisingly good listeners, if you want to talk.

Most important of all, they love you. That's why they're caring for you right now. They want to see you grow up well and happy, and they will do what they can to help you. And through their care and love they show the care of a loving God.

There are many good, kind, decent people in the world. Probably tops on your list are your family and your friends. As you grow up, you may find your relationship to them changing. But, through all the changes, you'll find that they remain good, kind, decent people.

You May Have Wondered

In this chapter you'll find explanations of words and phrases which you may have heard. All the words and phrases relate in some way to sex organs or sexual activities.

The explanations are listed alphabetically; they are not necessarily in order of importance. Who can say what's most important to you? You may be interested in a word or a phrase which your best friend doesn't care about at all. Or you may not be interested in any of this. The information is here because you may have wondered about it.

Abortion

Abortion is the removal of a developing baby from a mother's womb before it is time for that baby's birth. Some abortions are spontaneous (see miscarriage, p. 82). Other abortions are deliberate.

Doctors know how to give women abortions. Many doctors will not perform abortions, however, because they feel that they would be taking a human life.

Abortion is a very controversial issue. Most, but not all, sincere Christians believe that deliberate abortions are morally wrong.

This is an issue which you certainly must discuss with your parents and/or teachers.

Birth Control

The term *birth control* should really be "pregnancy control." It refers to precautions that a man and/or woman take to be sure that she won't become pregnant when they make love.

Although there are many different forms of birth control, no method is completely effective, except the practice of abstinence. The possibility of an unplanned pregnancy always exists.

Abstinence. To abstain means to completely avoid something or not to take part in some activity. If, during a conversation about sex, people say that they practice abstinence, they mean that they do not have sexual intercourse. Abstinence is a sure way to avoid pregnancy and, for both men and women, to avoid sexually transmitted diseases. When God tells us to avoid fornication and adultery, he's telling us to not have sex with anyone except the person to whom we are married. That rule is for our own good.

Condom. A condom is a stretchy, rubbery tube or sheath that a man puts over his penis before he has intercourse. It fits very snugly, but can expand considerably. When the man ejaculates, his semen is caught in the condom and is not released into the woman's vagina.

Some people use condoms to avoid getting a sexually transmitted disease. Because the condom covers the penis, the penis is never in direct contact with the woman's sexual parts. Using a condom is not a failproof precaution, however, because recent laboratory tests show that as many as twenty out of a hundred condoms are defective even when used correctly.

Diaphragm. A diaphragm is a dome-shaped rubber cap which a woman can insert into her vagina. It is designed to block the opening to her cervix. When sperm are released into the vagina, they are trapped there and can't fertilize an ovum waiting in a fallopian tube.

Pills. There are several types of birth control pills which a woman can take to avoid pregnancy. Most such pills contain synthetic ingredients that put her ovaries "to sleep" so they do not release an ovum each month.

Tubal ligation. Sometimes a woman will have her fallopian tubes cut and sealed shut so sperm cannot reach her ovum and she can't become pregnant.

Vasectomy. A man may have a vasectomy to prevent sperm traveling from his testicles to his penis. Because both vas deferens are cut and sealed shut, after a vasectomy there will be no sperm cells in a man's semen.

Caesarean Section

Sometimes it's difficult for a woman to give birth. The baby may be too big for the woman's birth canal (vagina). Or the baby may lie in an unusual position in the woman's womb. Most babies are born head first.

A doctor who knows that a woman will have a difficult delivery (it will be hard for the baby to be born naturally) may give her a Caesarean section. The doctor cuts through the woman's abdomen and the wall of her uterus. The baby can then be lifted out of the uterus instead of coming through the birth canal.

This operation is called a Caesarean section because, according to history, Julius Caesar was born this way. Sometimes it's simply called a C section.

A woman who has had a Caesarean section can have another baby.

Change of Life (Menopause)

When a woman becomes about forty-five or fifty years old, she gradually stops ovulating. This is called her change of life or menopause.

The change doesn't happen abruptly. Sometimes it happens gradually. A woman may not menstruate (because she has not ovulated) for a few months. Then she may have her period again. Finally, her period stops altogether because her ovaries stop releasing ova. She hasn't released all her ova. The remaining cells simply stay in her ovaries.

After a woman has had her change of life, she cannot become pregnant. She never has an ovum in her fallopian tubes, so no ovum can become fertilized. She can, however, still enjoy making love. She simply will not become pregnant.

Generally, having a baby is easier for a younger woman than for a woman of about fifty. A woman's menopause is God's way of protecting that woman. She won't be able to put too much strain on her body through a pregnancy and birth.

Conception

Conception is the process by which a woman becomes pregnant. After her ovum is fertilized, it travels through the fallopian tube and attaches itself to the wall of the uterus (womb).

After this happens, hormone signals stop menstruation so that the uterine lining (with the embryo embedded in it) isn't shed. The embryo grows within the womb and receives all the nourishment it needs through the uterine wall.

No one can say exactly how conception occurs. How a fertilized ovum "knows" that it must attach itself to the uterine wall remains a mystery.

Fertilization

Fertilization is the process by which a sperm enters an ovum, joins with it, and begins to form an embryo. This usually happens in the fallopian tube.

Many characteristics of a person are determined as soon as an ovum is fertilized. The sperm and the ovum each contain one half the information that will combine to form the new baby. This information comes in tiny units called genes. Although each cell is too tiny to be seen without a microscope, each contains thousands of genes which determine a person's skin color, hair color, eye color, nose shape, natural abilities, and many other things. The instant that a sperm and ovum combine, the fertilized ovum is on the way to becoming a unique person and yet a combination of two other people.

A person's sex is also determined at the moment of fertilization. Every ovum contains a sex chromosome (string of genes) called an X chromosome. Sperm cells contain either an X sex chromosome or a Y sex chromosome.

If a sperm containing an X sex chromosome fertilizes the ovum, the ovum will then have two X chromosomes, and a girl will develop. If a sperm containing a Y sex chromosome fertilizes the ovum, the ovum will then have an X and a Y chromosome, and a boy will develop.

No one can say exactly how a sperm "recognizes" an ovum to fertilize it or how the contents of the two cells "know" that they must merge. That's one of the mysteries of fertilization. Each cell contains one half the information necessary to begin a human life, and each cell seems to "recognize" this fact.

Homosexuality

You probably have heard people talk about homosexuals. They're also called gays (sometimes used to refer only to men), lesbians (used only of women), or some other terms. Homosexuals are individuals who find that they prefer, sexually, a person of the same sex as they are.

We can't tell if a person is homosexual simply by looking at him or her. A gay man isn't necessarily more feminine, nor is a lesbian necessarily more masculine.

The cause of homosexuality is not completely known. It may be the way a person is born, or it may be an incident or an upbringing which makes a person gay. We don't know for sure.

Almost every adult has, while he or she was maturing, felt strongly attracted to someone of the same sex. This doesn't mean that the person was a homosexual. It may have been a strong friendship developing, or a person's body coping with new hormones. After experiencing this same-sex attraction, most people keep friends of their sex, and develop attractions in a different way to the opposite sex. Homosexuals don't develop these attractions to the opposite sex.

Some homosexuals settle down with one partner into a marriage-type of relationship. Other homosexuals "play the field" and drift from one partner to the next.

Is homosexual activity wrong? Many Christians believe it is. God wants us to honor him with our bodies. That means we do not have an unlimited right to do as we please. They encourage the homosexual to exercise self-control and not engage in homosexual activity, just as the heterosexual should not practice fornication or adultery.

Hysterectomy

Sometimes a woman has medical problems with her uterus. If these problems are severe, a doctor may remove the uterus. This surgical removal of a uterus is called a hysterectomy.

A woman doesn't have her period after she has a hysterectomy. There's no uterus, so there's no lining to be shed.

Making Out

When people talk about petting, making out, or necking, they can be referring to almost any stage of becoming sexually involved with another person. There are all sorts of terms to describe this.

Generally, these terms don't refer to kissing only. But making out usually starts with kissing.

When a male and a female who are sexually mature (or becoming sexually mature) begin kissing each other, they generally don't want to stop. The next step is usually touching each other's sex organs and the woman's breasts. This makes them more excited, and they want to touch each other under their clothes. Or they may want to touch their sex organs together with or without clothes. Or they may want to masturbate each other. (This is called mutual masturbation.)

Any or all of these activities are referred to as petting, making out, necking, or by some other slang term.

All of this touching and kissing has an exciting physical effect on a person. Blood pours into the person's sex organs and she or he becomes flushed and breathes harder. Usually he or she wants to do more and more and get closer and closer to intercourse. When two people pet heavily, it's hard for them not to have intercourse. Every time they make out it becomes harder to stop before intercourse.

Some making out is natural between sexually mature men and women. God made us to be attracted to the opposite sex. Kissing and touching are the ways our bodies become ready for making love.

It's important to remember that sexual feelings can become strong. Heavy making out can be hard to stop and it can lead easily to sexual intercourse. But making love is special and involves more than just physical feelings, however strong and good those feelings are. God has told us that we should make love only with the person we have married.

Masturbation

When people masturbate, they play with their own sex organs until they have an orgasm. People usually masturbate when they are alone. Some, but not all, males and females masturbate. A male usually rubs his penis until he ejaculates. A female usually rubs her clitoris or vulva until she has an orgasm.

Masturbation usually gives a person the same physical feeling he or she would have while making love. But masturbation is only the physical feeling of one person alone. Making love involves two people and emotions as well as physical feeling.

Miscarriage

Sometimes, after a woman becomes pregnant, the fetus doesn't develop properly. When things begin to go wrong, the fetus (or the embryo) might break away from the uterine wall and be flushed from the woman's body. This is called a miscarriage or a spontaneous abortion.

The result of a miscarriage (spontaneous abortion) and a planned abortion are the same. The woman is no longer pregnant, but she probably can become pregnant again.

In a miscarriage, the woman can't control what happens. Her body flushes out a fetus (or an embryo) that wasn't developing properly. A miscarriage takes place automatically, beyond any person's control.

Multiple Births

Sometimes, during fertilization, there are more than one ovum in a woman's tubes. If there are more, usually there are two. If both these ova are fertilized (by two different sperm), twins will develop. Twins from two different fertilized ova are called fraternal twins.

Sometimes, after fertilization, one ovum develops into two separate babies. These are called identical twins. They developed from one sperm and one ovum, so they have identical genes.

At other times, more than two ova are fertilized at the same time. Triplets or quadruplets may develop. Or two ova may be fertilized and one may develop into identical twins. The third

Twins

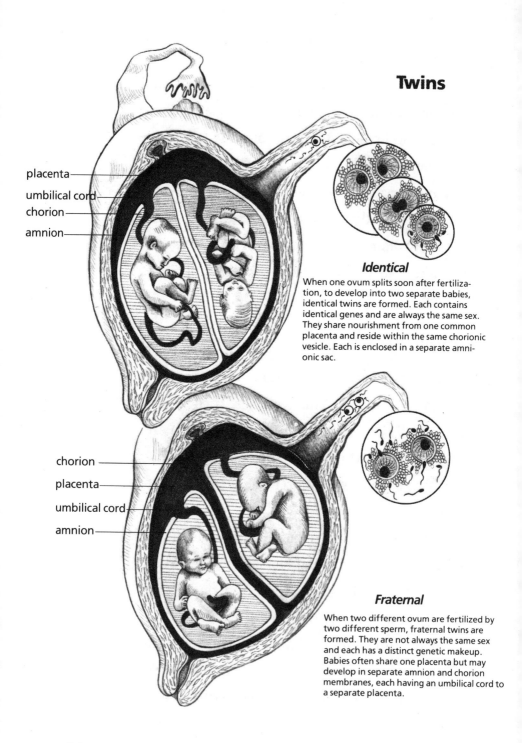

placenta
umbilical cord
chorion
amnion

Identical

When one ovum splits soon after fertilization, to develop into two separate babies,
identical twins are formed. Each contains
identical genes and are always the same sex.
They share nourishment from one common
placenta and reside within the same chorionic
vesicle. Each is enclosed in a separate amni-
onic sac.

chorion
placenta
umbilical cord
amnion

Fraternal

When two different ovum are fertilized by
two different sperm, fraternal twins are
formed. They are not always the same sex
and each has a distinct genetic makeup.
Babies often share one placenta but may
develop in separate amnion and chorion
membranes, each having an umbilical cord to
a separate placenta.

baby would be fraternal, but all three would be triplets.

If a woman takes a fertility drug (a drug to help her become pregnant), she sometimes has four or even five babies at one time. Fertility drugs often cause a woman to ovulate several ova at the same time. Multiple births in women who have not taken a fertility drug are quite rare.

Pregnancy and Birth

A human pregnancy lasts for about nine months. During this time the baby develops within the mother's womb, inside the amniotic sac (water sac). This sac is like a sealed bag filled with sweet clean water. The developing baby floats in this water, so it is protected from jarring and bumping.

The developing fetus is given the nourishment and the oxygen it needs through a special tube called an umbilical cord. This cord is attached to the placenta, a group of blood vessels which lies just outside the water sac, along the uterine wall. The mother's blood passes nourishment to the placenta. The placenta passes nourishment to the umbilical cord and on to the baby.

The development of a baby within a mother can be a long and amazing story. Each month the fetus grows and new body parts develop or grow. Each body part or organ develops at the right time, so that, within nine months, a whole human being is formed.

If you want to read about this development in detail, you should get a book from your library. We can list only a few of the stages of growth here.

After one month, the heart begins to beat.

After two months, the fetus is smaller than a thimble, yet it has two eyes, two ears, and all of its fingers and toes.

After four months, the fetus is about eight and one-half inches long. It has the beginnings of tiny eyelashes and eyebrows.

After seven months, the fetus has developed all the organs it will need, including a heart, lungs, and kidneys.

After nine months, the fetus is fully grown and ready to be born.

When it's time for the baby to be born, the amniotic sac breaks and the water drains through the mother's vagina. People refer to this as the water breaking. Then the walls of the uterus begin to contract, or push hard. This usually is painful for the mother, and is called labor pains.

The baby is pushed through the cervix, which has stretched open, and down through the vagina, which has also stretched. Usually a baby comes through the vagina, or birth canal, into the outside world head first. Sometimes a baby is born buttocks first. This is called a breech birth.

The placenta comes out shortly after the baby is born. The placenta is called the afterbirth.

After the baby is born, a doctor or someone helping the mother cuts the umbilical cord. This doesn't hurt because there are no nerves in the cord. The end of the cord which was attached to the baby dries and falls off. All that's left is the place where the cord was attached—the navel or the bellybutton. Now the baby must eat and breathe for itself.

During the last stages of pregnancy, a woman's breasts swell and fill with milk. This milk is the baby's first nourishment, unless the baby is bottle-fed. If a mother breast-feeds her baby, we say that she is nursing the baby.

It's easy to talk about pregnancy and birth, but it's hard to really understand. No one knows exactly what happens every day of a pregnancy

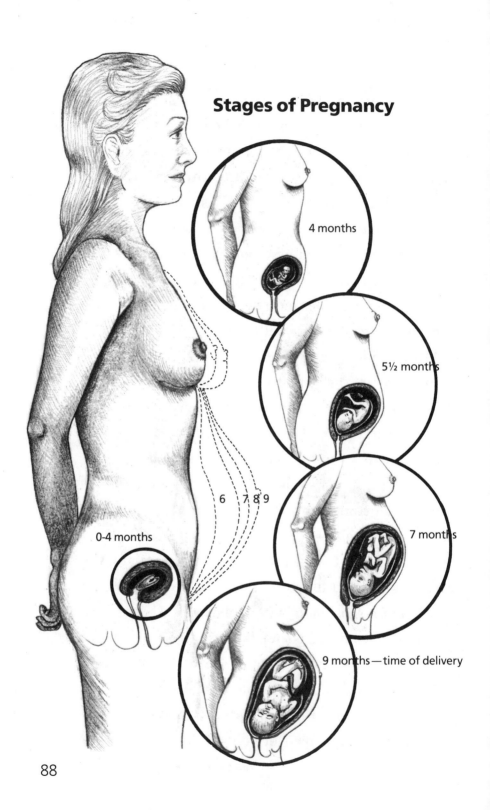

Stages of Pregnancy

4 months

5½ months

7 months

0-4 months

6 7 8 9

9 months—time of delivery

88

or exactly how the uterus "knows" when to start contracting. Pregnancy and birth is one of the most amazing wonders of our human bodies.

Safe Sex

You've probably heard a lot of talk about safe sex. When people use that phrase, they're talking about taking precautions to avoid getting a sexually transmitted disease from a partner during sexual activity.

Sexually Transmitted Diseases

Sexually transmitted disease (STD) is an infection which almost always is passed or transmitted from one person to another through sexual activity. Some STDs you may have heard mentioned are AIDS, chlamydia, gonorrhea, herpes, syphilis, and vaginitis. The infecting germs are carried in the body fluids—secretions from the vagina or penis, saliva, and in the case of AIDS, blood and perhaps tears.

Two people exchange body fluids when they engage in sexual activity, which in these cases includes not only all kinds of activity involving the sexual organs, but also activities with the mouth. Kissing, especially "deep" kissing, can transmit some of these diseases.

In many cases STDs are sneaky infections. Often a person who has an STD in an early stage might not know that he or she is infected. Yet that person can easily pass on the disease to another person who also will at first be unaware of the infection and so will not seek treatment.

Some STDs are not curable. If you get such a disease, you will have it for the rest of your life. While other STDs are curable, the scarring left by only one infection may leave a girl sterile, unable ever to become pregnant. Others involve bothersome and painful sores at the beginning stages and seem to disappear for a time only to return with bone damage, cardiovascular damage, and even death. A pregnant woman with an untreated STD can at times do great damage to her fetus.

Usually people are checked for STDs by a doctor before they get married. If neither the man nor the woman has an STD, neither will get one if they have sexual activity with only their spouse. Again, the warning against adultery and fornication is for our own good.

AIDS, however, is a different story. Everyone knows that it is a fatal disease which we cannot cure. It is transmitted mainly by sexual activity but it can also be passed in blood. Sometimes people have received AIDS-infected blood in a transfusion. Drug users who share needles can pass the AIDS virus to each other. The warning against "doing drugs" takes on special urgency here. It can mean death.

Surprise Babies

Sometimes a family will have one child who is much younger than the others. This child is often called a "surprise," a "trailer," a "caboose," or one of many other terms. You probably have heard some different terms.

This child usually was a surprise because the parents thought that, for some reason, the mother could not become pregnant. Her pregnancy, not the birth, was the surprise.

If you're a "trailer" or a "surprise," ask your parents about it some time. They'll probably tell you that the pregnancy was a surprise, but that you weren't when you arrived. By that time they were looking forward to your arrival. They'll probably tell you that, now that you are here, you're special to them.

Test-Tube Babies

Test-tube babies were not grown in test tubes. They simply had their beginnings there.

Sometimes, for a medical reason, a woman can't become pregnant. A doctor will then take one of her ova and fertilize it with her husband's sperm in a test tube. The fertilized ovum is then put into the woman's womb. It develops normally within the womb and is born normally.

The baby is called a test-tube baby only because the ovum was fertilized in a test tube rather than in a fallopian tube.

You may have heard a word or a phrase that was not mentioned in this chapter. If you have and you wonder what that word or phrase means, ask one of your parents or a teacher about it. They'll probably be glad that you asked, and happy to explain things to you. They were young once, too, and probably wondered about some of the same things. There's no sense in wondering, when a simple question can bring you the answers.

Sexuality and the Young Christian

In Conclusion . . .

You may have noticed that we haven't used slang in this book. No slang terms appear in the glossary.

You will hear slang. You probably already have. People use all sorts of words when they talk about sexual intercourse, a vulva, a penis, or anything relating to sex.

These words change from time to time and from place to place. Different people use different slang terms. Certain words are used commonly and most people understand them.

You should know the meaning of the slang terms you hear for your own good. If you don't, people could make improper comments to you and you wouldn't know what they're talking about.

When you hear a slang term that you don't understand, ask a parent or a teacher about it.

They'll be happy to tell you what that term means and what's the right word instead of the slang.

The fact that you will understand slang terms doesn't mean that you should use them. Why use a vulgar, offensive, childish term when you know the right word? Why make something as beautiful as sex sound so crude?

People who use slang reveal how they feel about sex and their sexuality in the way they talk. Sometimes they're embarrassed about sex; they're afraid to use words like "sexual intercourse" openly. Sometimes they think that sex is "dirty," so they snicker and use "dirty" words. They don't really understand what sex and their sexuality are all about.

You've understood, probably since you were a young child, that God made you and God loves you. He cares for you and he wants you to be happy and enjoy life.

God has given you many gifts. Every day of your life he gives you the ability to think, to talk, to play, and to laugh. He's given you a wonderful, responsive body. That's cause for celebration! He's given you love and many ways to express your love. And he's given you an especially beautiful gift in sex and your awakening sexuality.

Glossary

The definitions given in this glossary are not necessarily complete definitions. They define how the words are used in this book. For example, the word *erection* can have several definitions. Some of those definitions have no relationship to sexual activities. The only definition given here is that which applies to our discussion.

The number which appears after each definition refers to the page on which that word is first found. Definitions which have no numbers behind them are not mentioned elsewhere in the book. They are included here in case you want the definition.

Words which are discussed in the chapter "You May Have Wondered" are not defined again in the glossary.

Acne (AK nee) A condition of the skin, characterized by pimples. (50)

Adolescent (Ad ō LES sent) A person who is becoming an adult.

Adultery (a DULL ter ee) Sexual intercourse between a married person and someone other than that person's husband or wife. (42)

Breast (BREST) An enlarged female gland, on the upper part of her torso, which is capable of producing milk for her baby. (51)

Cervix (SIR vicks) The narrow lower end of the uterus which opens into the vagina. (32)

Circumcision (sir kum SIH shun) The removal of the foreskin from a penis. (22)

Clitoris (KLIT oh ris) A small, sensitive female sex organ located within the vulva. (34)

Ejaculation (ee jack you LAY shun) The spurting of semen out of a penis. (25)

Embryo (EM bree ō) An unborn baby in its first eight weeks of development.

Epididymis (ep eh DID ih miss) A tube, behind the testicle, which stores sperm and produces some liquid. (20)

Erection (ee REK shun) The stiffening and swelling of a penis. (24)

Fallopian tube (fah LŌ pee un) A tube which extends from an ovary to the uterus. Also called an oviduct. (29)

Fetus (FEE tus) An unborn baby which has developed for eight weeks or more.

Foreskin (FOUR skin) A fold of skin which covers the tip of a penis. (22)

Fornication (four ni KĀ shun) Sexual intercourse on the part of an unmarried person. (42)

Genitals (JEN i talz) The external, visible sex organs. (53)

Homosexual (hō mō SEX u al) A person who prefers another person of the same sex for sexual activities. (78)

Hormone (HOR moan) A chemical message produced by a gland and carried in the blood. (49)

Hymen (HI men) The fold of skin which partially covers a vaginal opening. (35)

Incest (IN sest) Sexual intercourse with a blood relative. (67)

Menstruation (men stru Ā shun) The periodic discharge of blood, tissue, and secretions from the uterus through the vagina. (36)

Molesting (mō LES ting) Physically handling a person, especially that person's sex organs, against that person's will. Harming a person in some way. (66)

Orgasm (OR gaz um) A climax or peak of sexual excitement. (25)

Ovary (Ō va ree) A female sex organ in which egg cells develop. (27)

Ovulate (AH vū late) To release a mature egg cell from an ovary. (37)

Ovulation (AH vū lā shun) The act of releasing a mature egg cell from an ovary. (37)

Ovum (Ō vum) A female egg cell. (28)

Penis (PEE nis) The male organ through which both urine and semen pass out of the body. (21)

Pornography (pour NOG ruh fee) Writing or pictures which offend a person's sense of decency.

Prostitute (PROS tih toot) A person who has sexual intercourse for money.

Puberty (PŪ bur tee) That time of life in which a person first becomes sexually mature. When a girl first begins to ovulate or a boy begins to produce sperm.

Pubic (PŪ bik) Of or relating to the region around the external sex organs. (53, 57)

Rape The act of forcing a person to have sexual intercourse. (66)

Scrotum (SKRŌ tum) A sac of skin which contains the testicles. (17)

Semen (SEE men) A sticky, whitish liquid which contains sperm cells. (21)

Seminal emission (SEM ih nal ee MISH un) The releasing of semen from the body.

Seminal vesicle (SEM ih nal VES i kal) A gland which makes liquid for semen and pours it into a vas deferens. (20)

Sex The state of being male or female; relating to certain male-female activities. (11)

Sexuality (sex you AL ih tee) Maleness or femaleness; the state of being sexual; sexual abilities. (63)

Sperm A male reproductive cell which is capable of fertilizing a female egg cell. (16)

Testicles (TES tih kals) The male sex glands which produce sperm cells. (16)

Urethra (u REE thra) A tube which conducts urine from the bladder outside the body. In males the urethra also conducts semen. (21, 35)

Uterus (U ter us) A hollow, pear-shaped female organ for protecting and nourishing a developing embryo or fetus. Also called the womb. (29)

Vagina (va JĪ na) The passage which leads from the uterus to the vulva in a female body. Also called the birth canal. (33)

Vaginal opening (VAH je nal) The entrance to the vagina, located within the vulva. (35)

Vas deferens (vas DEF er ens) A tube which conducts sperm cells from the epididymis to the urethra. Also called a sperm duct. (20)

Virgin (VER jin) A person who has not had sexual intercourse.

Vulva (VUL va) The external female sex organs. (34)